NEWS FROM THE SOUTH

News from the South

1. FIVE A.M.

Now is the hour of the Sunday morning paper.
The motorcycle comes, and then the throw
Of the hard headlines. It breaks a window. So
I get the word, being a light sleeper.
There's always some bad news I have to know.
I am, inevitably, my brother's keeper.

2. THE CRAZY PREACHER

You see that flight of hawks? he said: they're straight
Out of Ovid's Metamorphoses. There fly
Ritual rape and subterfuge and hate.
I mean it. When you see them in the sky
Like that, racing up, up, in such a state,
There's been a massacre somewhere, a lie
Found out, a cross burned at someone's gate.

When the gods get angry, suddenly a man-cry
Becomes a screaming bird-voice. You have to die
If you think fate means being others' fate.
But you return. Then you rise very high
And see the place itself become your omen:

Grim birds, dishonored men and women,
The soul of every hawk was once a human.

3. THE SENTIMENTAL CIRCUS-BARKER

"Who is this lady all in gold and green
Satin, with sequins, glittering hollow-eyed?
The junior miss, the maid of cotton, the corn-queen?"

This is that same poor dame who tried but died
When she saw something that she hadn't seen:

Herself in a mirror, propped up stiff, between
Two servants, female cousins, whose unclean
Kinship was more than she could bear. She tried,
Puzzle-headedly, to see: "What do you mean,"
She hedged, "I'm dead?" But she was mystified
Not knowing what to know. And then a lean
Asylum-keeper came and got her. Pride
Kept her from falling. When she stood there and died,
Erect, without a tremor in her hands,
They sold her to the circus. There she stands,
On her own feet.
                        Nobody treats her rough,
The pretty lady who couldn't know enough.

4. PHILADELPHIA, MISSISSIPPI

It didn't matter to them when the shovel
Of the bull-dozer started; they had lost
Consciousness already—such rites are civil
Enough if you are dead.
                          But feel the thrust
Of mounds of moving mud and sand and gravel
Bury your bones to make a dam hold fast.

So the night's violence, the day's upheaval
Shudder in the imagination of a ghost
Who died before this sequel to his novel
Returned three more intruders to the dust.

5. THE MAD JUDGE METES OUT PUNISHMENT

Force them to look up and up and up at the stars.
Tie them down like Gulliver on their backs,
A mile apart. Let silence break their hearts.
Teach them astronomy if they can learn
What kind of prison space is. Let them cry.

6. A BOMBING IN BIRMINGHAM

One month after. Soon will come
  Two, and then the time will be
  A year ago, at length a century
And a quaint, archaic millennium.

And still we call this foreign country home.

7. A BLACK CHILD SINGING

The songs of boys are wild and rough
Their sisters' wild and witty
Grandfathers' songs are grim and gruff
Grandmothers' prim and pretty.

But the sounds I listen for most of all
In the string- and drum- and horn-
Prophecies we play are those that call
To the child that never was born.

8. THE CRAZY PREACHER AGAIN

How can that mocking-bird fail to distinguish
A hawk-shriek from a thrush-call? How can he
Cry jay, cry cardinal, cry joree?
He never had Tereus to teach him anguish.
But he will learn it. Let him sing and see.

After Selma

. . . the knife-order.
—T. E. Hulme

Let him lie sober when he tells the lie
That horror has no times to match these times.
The warning is a storm in his own eye.

We have a sign to follow in the sky,
With flags and triggers, to protect our dreams.
Let him lie sober when he tells the lie.

Bars-sinister and -dexter mortify
Visiting pilgrims who commit no crimes;
The warning is a storm in his own eye.

This land will bury you before you die,
Bombard your churches and blast out your homes.
Let him lie sober when he tells the lie.

Whoever wounds you must consent to buy
Silence, a scar-tissue of wordless names.
The warning is a storm in his own eye.

Discarded winding-sheets will tell you why
We meet the dead in living pantomimes.
 Let him lie sober when he tells the lie.
 The warning is a storm in his own eye.

A Kentuckian and a Virginian in Alabama

Not quite a pastoral: the year almost gone,
Leaves wrestling over the pavement, a wild sky, and
A liberal and a poet on the lawn
Of the library, arguing with the wind;
Or slanting into it, their topcoats flown
Thin and billowing: Tate and Jenkins, blond
Saxon and red Welsh, two men in the afternoon
Like leaves. And there, immobile, they still stand:

Two leaves, forever buffeted in a brisk
And Southern wind that can not find
A way to move, nor the direction it should ask
Of them, to move . . .
                    Guardian of the Wind
That wrestles whom It pleases, guard these leaves
Safely to where they were going all their lives.

The Flag

Her sky was a flag. Her stars, like anthems, sang
Each to the other upon a cloth of blue.

And yet she saw flowing from it seven strains
Of native blood, with bandages—six brave new
Parallels of purity—unfurling in between.

But she was making stars, and found it good.
What if she had pricked her fingers twice thirteen
Times?
      Suddenly her needle stopped. How could
Those flying bandages soak up so much blood?
How long would the stars keep bleeding? And how long
Before those five-pointed anthems understood
What dreams they were, how many they stood among?

She wept. She dried her tears on the flag.
                        There fly
Her fingers, sewing anthems, in the sky.

Bread and Wine

After the Lenten purges came the plague:
Sometime the Furies, and sometime the flat
Gray fall of air into a dinner-plate,
Bland as the news-announcer's monologue.
These ashes were the malady, the drug
We drank to cure it, and the delicate
Relief of thirst: the knowledge that we ate
To starve the Furies battening on the fog.

Tuesday and Wednesday and then forty days
Past Carnival, we took the Eucharist
Again. Bread of this earth, Wine of the Skies,
Were you transformed, or did you leave the ways
Of consubstantiation to the mist
That, if we eat or drink it, crucifies?

THE GARDEN

Water Color

There are some quiet crossings in his city
  Where the wind holds up red kites
    In a sky of flaky whitewash.
  The roads are black, like roads
    Drawn brusquely by a child.

Then suddenly the child decides that roads
  And kites are not enough; there must
    Be grass along the roads,
  And there is grass. But this is red
    Grass, in windy weather.

Grass calls for sun, a red swirl in between
  The kites, which now require a boy
    To hold the strings. His jacket
  And shoes and trousers must be red.
    All red he draws himself.

The roads are brusque and black because
  It has been raining. In skies like these,
    The wind can quickly bring another
  Rain. So comes at once oblique
    Black rain into the whitewashed sky.

The black rain mixes with the white,
  And a wet-gray, rosy sky consumes
    The sodden roads and kites,
  Consumes the rain itself, dissolves the child
    Who stands at the quiet crossing,

And a sheet of paper, solid gray, floats
On the water, which is also gray.

Names

The names we fear are always misconceived
Spectres—an empty bed, an unlocked door.
The only horror is not being loved.

We name our ruins, as if lists removed
Mountains of unfaith, when we knew before
The names we fear are always misconceived.

In spite of any dangers we have lived,
Or loss defined, or dust we may explore,
The only horror is not being loved.

Say that the earth's gone bad, the air depraved,
The moral climate turned to grime and gore.
The names we fear are always misconceived.

Reality's a hope that's never proved.
We name it with illusions and no more.
The only horror is not being loved.

Names are beloved because they are believed.
There is some charity we can restore.
  The names we fear are always misconceived.
  The only horror is not being loved.

The Garden

There is no evidence. But here was a marriage
In which the husband killed the wife—sometimes
It goes the other way. It took him several years
Industriously pushing her ankle-deep
Into the greensward of the formal garden
While she, resisting statuesquely, grew genteel
Under the neighbors' eyes. "In fact, it's not
Unpleasant here," she sighed, and the ground rose up
Two inches higher on her legs.

       Nobody could dispute
That she was courteously cared for. Day after day
The clocks chimed on the landings of three flights
Of stairs, each waiting until the last one finished
To let the masculine bass bells sound one by one
Through open windows, clearly. Nourishing meals
Were brought to her on time.

       Naturally
She was bathed at night, after the moon went down.
Sometimes, faintly, someone passing
On the other side of the hedge would think he saw
The husband making love to her, and pause
To watch their shadows wrestle darkly, forming
A kind of fire that gives no light. The leaves
Would rustle, and the stranger would steal on,
Moved by faint expectations.

       One night she sank
Into the ground well past her knees; and now
She could touch the grass without bending over,

Feeling it under her fanned-out palms
Like close-cropped human hair. From this time on
She liked her situation better: As she learned
To hope for nothing, to remember nothing,
As she learned at last to wait, the trip down
Went faster. At once the legless torso
—Her husband's hands faithfully at her shoulders—
Became a bust, a head, a frontal bone,
A lost curl of hair. The final push
Happened in full day, when the lawn-sprinklers
Were making showers of wet light. Three birds
Flew through the spray, and rapid rainbows
Whirled all the light away.

                        Far off, the cockatoos
    Cried in the warning jungle. Fish
    Nibbled algae in the fragile ponds;
    And carelessly among remote Gibraltars
    Submerged in the Atlantic, a school
    Of eels swam through an open door
    Under a steep escarpment, out of mind.

Frost

Always a poem lying down behind
Him,
And handsomer than he,
His shadow, silence of his other mind.

Or striding in the sun, deepening
The color of the grass,
Transforming a tree
—Whatever this tall shadow touched would bring
Itself to pass,
Go blind
To itself, begin to be
A creature of his make; begin to wind
Into a new existence, now and then
In space, a miracle without a plan.

Sestina

FOR CAROLYN STEELE

When a little girl, one year old,
Walks on her toes, she is already
Wearing finery and high heels.
She is barefoot, of course,
And the kitchen floor is cold.
This is the best part of the morning.

She ignores the marvel of the morning:
Pear-blossoms, bride-white, on the old
Tree by the window, against a cold
Flag-stone sky. The sun is up already.
Gowned like a bride, she takes her course
Around the kitchen, on elevated heels,

Promising to dance. Can such heels
Lift her enough to see the morning
Sun in its finery? She stuffs coarse
Rags of toast in my pockets. I am old
Enough now to love her schemes—already
Her eyes are dancing, changing, cold

As the sky. I have to take the cold
Toast out. The silence of her heels
Goes round the room. The pear-tree's ready

To make such vows to the spring morning
That she will bloom even when she is old.
At this point the sun is changing course.

It puts a window on the floor. Of course
She walks across it, and the cold
Begins to vanish in a shape as old
As walls and warmth. I know that my heels
Are wingless, vulnerable. In the morning
A child is a wound like the sun. Unready,

Unwilling to let myself be ready
To see the window turn its course
To the ceiling, I swear that some morning
When she asks me I'll tell her that the cold
Is nothing more than a shadow at the heels
Of a pear-tree, blooming because it is old.

She laughs at me. Now she is ready
To ride my foot, around the oldest racecourse
On the heels of a beautiful cold morning.

Cheiron

FOR ERIC STOCKTON

Ixion in your wheel-chair,
Still young, centaur undone,
Your guilt made visible, your bravery
Exposed: I love you better
For the grace your gestures show,
Your rash ambition now fallen
To match the burdens of that beast
Whose mysterious disease you bear.

Your rigid love for the forbidden
Goddess has numbed your knees to a slow
Climb across horizontal space.
The wheels that are your feet
Turn in these years to face the fire
That warms you toward the being you desire.

Young Swimmers

When we knew nothing but the bluejay's feather,
Acres of wooded sunlight, and generations
Of birds shouting their ancestry together
In fields where causes proved their own occasions;
When water was all the wisdom of the diver,
The surface poised to meet the clean delivery
Of the boy into his picture, and up, and over,
Whetting his knife-like body for what bravery?—

Then we knew music, for we were a rhythm
Of scythe and scissors working to no design
But the rush of mirrors in a downward fathom,
Ourselves the plummet and the sounding-line:
Then in ultimate summer the healing ways
Of images commanded all our days.

A Zodiac

FOR JULIA STOCKTON

The sky is an enormous cage
Which I suppose is in a zoo
Of sorts, which must be at the edge
Of a park that people can walk through

To feed the animals. The bear
Though he seems amiable is not.
On the contrary, the centaur,
No matter what you may have thought,

Is gentle and quite beautiful,
Poising an arrow in his bow,
Perhaps to frighten off the bull,
The lion, and the ram also.

You will be careful, but it's best
To stand off at a distance. Then
You're safe. And you should not request
That the attendant let you in,

For everyone who ever tried
Has said it's pleasanter outside.

The Guide's Speech

To be a successful apparition
It is necessary to remember
Three things: Always be slightly late.
Be tangible in a few expert ways.
And, most of all, believe: Always believe
That you are real.
                   Have a real face,
With eyes. And hands, each hand uniquely
Veined; the patterns must not match.
Some evidence of struggle, a personal mark,
A scar on the thumb or at the edge
Of the cheek-bone will be persuasive,
                   Stimulating
Images of falls in childhood and normal
Adolescent accidents with knives.
Pay no attention to your feet.
                   Walk—do not run.

The inner organs do not matter in our usual
Public appearances; they will be assumed.
Expand your clothing to its proper curve

And line. Bend, bow, and kneel. Everyone
Will think you a sensible creature,
Pouched with life, rounded and bounded
And bagged and bundled with life.
                    So designed,
You may descend to find what you shall find.

POETRY IS PERCUSSION

Poetry is Percussion

Come off your sweet things and explore
Gambles and wrecks. It's time we heard
The quicksticks and the whackos more.

Who says a skin must be a score
Dancing the drybones? Dying's absurd.
Come off your sweet things and explore

Auroras. Twilight's a ghastly bore.
You might ask rare birds why and here's the word:
The quicksticks and the whackos more

And more crack padlocks and spring the jail-door
Open. When the gong goes in the circus-yard
Come off your sweet things and explore

Crescendos. Jungles know how to roar
And cages roar even when locked and barred.
The quicksticks and the whackos, more

Than hushing brushes can, strike up the air
As kindling wood scores candles out of sticks.
It is the phoenix we're on fire for
Since Herakleitos first put wax on wicks.

A Gothic Tale

FOR KENNETH CURRY

[*Some years after the interment of
Robert Burns, the mausoleum was
opened to receive the remains of his
wife. Phrenologists from the Edin-
burgh Phrenological Society, di-
rected by Dr. Algernon Blacklock,
joined the mourners, taking advantage of the occasion to measure
the poet's skull and make a plaster
cast of it for study.*]

When Doctor Blacklock saw Jean Armour Burns
Resting below her husband in the stiff
Decorum of the tomb, it looked as if
The scandal would at last yield joint-returns.

Clergy and kin, honored phrenologists,
They came to bid farewell to Burns's spouse;
Husband and wife received as ghosts their guests
And in their mausoleum kept open house.

The mourners in a candle-lit charade
Combined their grief with honest Gothic dreams
Of figuring, by phrenologic deed,
The landscape of the poet's toponyms.

Item, Sublimity, the depth and height
Of feeling. Item, Combativeness, the source
Of power. Item, the poet's whole delight,
Amativeness, his genius and force;

For here the soul undoubtedly would yield
Its truth: the poet in the peasant crowned,
The latter a fashionable farmer in the field
Of dialect, the former's proving-ground.

So expectation touched the Doctor's heart.
Why should not Poetry confirm his faith?
But truth lives by obedience to art;
A scientist, he had to tell the truth.

A textbook maxim had the circumstance
Nicely, precisely put, with Gothic grace:
*A prominent occipital protuberance
Signifies: Philoprogenitiveness.*

—What could the Doctor hope to harvest now?
The skull's geography was frank and rude.
It was an honest crag of Fatherhood
Had kept the farmer at the lover's plow.

And what of Amativeness? It was small.
Under the scanty iron-gray chevelure,
The Doctor felt and found the true contour:
Poetry's the love of offspring, after all.

The funeral was over. From the mourning farms
Old women remembered the peasant-poet's arms.

The Middle Age of a Traveling Salesman

I met a salesman in a song,
 With hey! the sweet birds over the dale,
And asked him how he plied his trade,
What tales he told, what tricks he sprung,
And whether he'd ever been in jail.
"Only in jail in love," he said.
—*In heaven's cage with hell's own rage.*

"The way we did when I was young
Was starlight, carlight, rockabye-bye:
Anyboobaby, in the back seat,
Sang the radio song, or Who or Why,
Like birds in the woods, the nights were sweet.
When lovers were leavers O how they clung!"
—*Turning and burning by light-years' light.*

"And over these ever-loving years
Taking lovers and trading them in
And making my life a rolling store
I've had twelve dozen dozen dears."
He boasted, but when he spoke again
His voice grew sterner than before.
—*In heaven's cage with hell's own rage.*

"The bird that tirra-lirra trills
—A summer song in a winter's tale—
Mocks me, mocks me! The thrush and the jay
Sing, years of gears and steering wheels
Will come and steal your love away.

Jealousy-fallacy, life's a deal."
—*Turning and burning by light-years' light.*

And how does it go in middle age?
"With a thickening, blackening spot in the eye.
It's wheels all week, fall day, fall night,
But say what you will do never say die."
—*Turning and burning by light-years' light*
  In heaven's cage with hell's own rage.

Dancing in Circles

The dancers are the music. Turning round
  The clock,
      the moon,
           the drum,
                 they turn
The circle of themselves, a sound
  That makes a substance. They are born
To hear the clock sing and the drum tell
The moon's time in the trumpet-bell.

It is themselves they go to meet,
  To form another image of
  The dancing algebra of love.
The drummer holds them to their fate.
  His fugue's a pulse, a calculus,
    A full placenta for the sounds
      Of headlong metamorphosis.
    The forceps of his furious hands
Deliver eyes and cries and feet,
    And then a gradual caress.

  The digits of the circle sing
Seek and go hide. The blind-buff's touch
  As on a combination lock
Tumbles along the dial ring
  —A telephone, a safe, a clock—
Until the timeless numbers match,

39

Making the moon itself clang one.
  It is because there is a wand
Directs the drummer's undertone.
  The moon's a cymbal in his hand.

And if the rumors of the night
  Hold nothing new for his regard,
Something is being brought to light.
  The whole world's an obstetrics ward.

On My Way to the Circus

Nobody will be surprised to hear
That on my way to the circus long ago
I fell in with Mary Allen (a primrose)
And held her hand in church; I feel
The dew of her primroses still.
                                On the other hand,
It seems absurd that Dolores Dubonnet
(A tigress) should be remembered
                        For her feet,
Which she handled with sinister ambi-
                        Dexterity.

  She could write with her toes,

Holding a pencil there as easily as I hold one
In my fingers. She was feline, svelte—in short,
A tigress manquée on a Persian carpet. And,
What is more, she could at the same time write
With both her left hand and her right,

  Simultaneously, upside-down and backwards.
It was necessary to hold the manuscript or
Pediscript the wrong way in the mirror, to get it
Right; and when you had it fixed correctly,
                        What you saw (in
Flawless Palmer Method) was *Ontogeny*
                Recapitulates Phylogeny,
And other such popular tags and straws,

To which inadequacy clings, whether by
                    Left hand or foot or right
                    Hand or foot, or all four.
This was indeed the finest feat
Of using oneself in a complete way
That I ever saw, surpassing in fact
                    The Great Pipe Organ
                    Of the 'thirties
(Five-manualed, multi-stopped, thaumaturgic),
That pulsed and puddled with a peacock
                    Iridescence, showing how
Peristaltic-action-pastels assimilate Direct
Current opaquely behind distended celluloid.
                    However, the exquisite
Muscular coördination of Dolores Dubonnet
Was rendered somewhat fearsome by its
                    Similarity to the fugal
Assaults on chastity in Pierre Louys, q.v.
Dolores, with her sad and drinking name,
                    Was wildly sober,
                    Like a sorceress.
At last she was captured and put in a cage
                    By an Act of Congress, to wit,
Her husband's family. She became right-handed,
And walked on a deep-piled wall-to-wall carpet,
A mother to grown children. Yet to this day
                    I feel a certain rage,
Seeing how even a sorceress will age.

Orpheus to Eurydice

Before the long winter and the helter-skelter
   Hocus-pocusing of sheer abracadabra,
      Let me return to you, O Zoo
In Alabama, where the skies tilt;
And the demented tiger and the gnu
And Jarrell's eland and nobody's cobra
      Glare when the food arrives.
On to the western mock-up. There the zebra
         With his wives
Displays a great erection (it is not
       Striped, by the way) ;
Past the mad leopard pacing in his hot
Grot of concrete—his spouse today
Brought forth three young in the obstetrics ward,
       All spotted like the pard.
      Then on to watch the polar bears
        Stretch, fetch, and roll
     Through counterfeit careers
        At a counterfeit North Pole.

For there, dreaming, below the drink-
      Stand, near the bears
      (It makes me sink to think
About it), sits a girl who wears
The tightest god-almighties, screaming
       To be picked up, before
Kill-joy cracks down and desolates the zoo.
      By the caged tiger's roar,
That which I should have done I did not do!

Miss America Gets a Little Old

There she goes in her shell-pink Caddy;
Her eyes are skies and her hair is gold.
She buys it and dyes it to please her daddy,
A rich arthritic, but not too old.

Cruising through edible californias
Of TV houses with no back doors
Those eyes like skies see nothing but menus.
The drain pipes are clean and the vodka pours.

She measures her sands and her ocean frontage
And sells by the inch—it's the last shore-line
Of its flavor there, a sharp advantage
When a girl wants the drink without the brine.

I'll be buried, she sighed, in a glass mausoleum
Till reincarnation returns my soul
To Los Angeles.—Now she's getting per diem
In heaven to leaven sweet daddy's bank roll.

The Luxembourg Gardens Blues

O the bad boys with their burdens,
   The sad girls past their prime
Sing the blues in the Luxembourg Gardens
   Practically all the time.

And the stars like a national anthem
   Sing down in the minor mode:
—Our influences if you could count them
   Would drive you dancing mad:

Frère Jacques has gone to pot,
   Françoise has lost her looks;
Little Dick and Jane are not
   What they were in the story books.

Old Hans writhes on the arse
   Of his tatterdemalion jeans.
It's a question of what to rehearse
   In the battle of ends and means.

And the ding-dong dads with a failing
   Shrink up in their inner-tubes
When Mammary Mae comes rolling
   Those once remarkable boobs.

45

When the native blues turn foreign,
  It's a nightmare chasing a dream.
You can bring a new beat to the bar in,
  But it's Saint Louis just the same.

Late summer's a bad example
  Of Eden to show to the young.
Look under the leaves of the apple,
  The boughs are not very well hung.

—Over here in the uninventive
  Half light the voyeurs steal.
The pigeons are cooing, attentive
  To the statue of Leconte de Lisle.

O the stars in their scar-cursed courses
  Are calling it a day.
The girls with low-slung purses
  Move on to the Champs-Elysées.

And midnight falls with the calm
  Of an eyesocket struck by a fist.
The tourists have headed back home
  And the gates are all locked fast.

In a Southern Classroom

EXPLORATION OF A CLUE BY ORTEGA Y GASSET

1

And now, my students, we have a demonstration,
This time in American, of the didactic tone,
Such as Ortega, if he could face the nation,
Might do by radio, TV, or telephone.

2

Creation's a pyramid. Just at the top
The Few produce, for sheer creation's sake.
The Many, who consume, mutter, "What's up?"
Sometimes the answer comes out best in Greek.

3

"But isn't this the end of an age, according
To the cyclic historians? And what are we living for?"
—Look twice at fine apocalyptic wording,
And question even the aptest metaphor.

4

The Odyssey still works, though; Homer uncovered
The archetype, and the copies go on and on.
Stout Cortez, for example; Keats delivered
Him to us, and James made him American.

47

5

Very well: Question. "What helpful message
Would the great Spaniard have for the South today?"
—"Stop celebrating ghostly rites of passage;
Get out of the grave, throw the winding-sheet away."

6

(Chuckles and raised eyebrows.) The Southern Trauma,
A hundred-year-old nightmare, and well-named,
Could probably be cured by a strong Program of Drama;
Pity and terror keep the wild will tamed.

7

And, again, there's Meliorism: a way of life
Invented and re-invented, like a dance.
Effort is dangerous, but inertia's not safe
Either. Gamble; take a dancer's chance.

8

Start with the Lower, not with the Higher Passions.
—Time's running out. But here's one maxim more:
"To change a man, change his identifications;
To change a region, you must change its lore."

9

Drama's the way the human will corrects
Illusion: That's what reality is all about,
Tentatively. "But what will happen next?"
Secrets. And whispers. And then a mighty shout.

10

MORAL

Wrestle with life, with death, but do not live
For safety's sake; think, love, forgive.

The Piano Tuner

For mem'ry has painted this perfect day
      With colors that never fade.
                    —*C. J. B.*

"I want to be like Carrie Jacobs Bond,"
    Aunt Stella said in earnest and sat down
    at her piano and, oh, she was—she was
identical in size and similarly gowned,
      the means and end of culture in our town
      who made the music and imposed the laws
of taste. And of C major she was queen.
    One perfect day, when she was fairly glued
    to her piano, the tuner walked right in

and started tuning while she played: a scene
—of love? of war? or something in between?
    Still, in C major, rapidly ensued
    cacophony and crime. It was a sin,

such atonality, such eighth- and sixteenth-tones
    the tuner twisted into those sweet wires.
    When Stella touched crescendos, she was manic;
with fifty fingers, she stuck by her guns
    while the piano tuner twisted choirs
    of caterwaulings, parrots in a panic,
canaries in cadenzas. With both hands,
    that wizard drove them all into the key
    of C major. The old piano roared.

I hate to bring bad tidings to my friends
   but those who make such music finally
   may lose their wits indeed, all kind accord
   of black with white along the full keyboard.
Nurse may entreat and doctor give commands
   (sedation and no music, certainly),
   but only the mildest cases can be cured.

Time that corrodes the tuner's fork still sings
of Carrie's day and Stella's jangled strings.
   The foolish song runs out. The moral's plain:
   Too simple music cannot stand the strain.

Strange Bedfellows:
Procrustes on Politics

Two tricks, one short, the other tall,
Were telling fancies to a wall.
The first one to the other said,
   "If I could spend one hour with you,
   I'd exercise my power with you."
The second to the first replied,
"No. I could take you in my stride."
   I put them in a double bed
   And made them wish that they were dead.

LETTER FROM IRELAND

The headpiece of each section is an adaptation from Bartholomew Anglicus' De Proprietatibus Rerum *(c. 1250),* Trevisa's translation, 1397; edition of Berthelet, 1535.

Letter from Ireland

Yrlonde hight Hibernia, and is an island
Of the Ocean in Europe, and is nigh
To the land of Britain, and is more narrow
And straight than Britain, but it is
More plenteous place. In this land
Is much plenty of corn fields, of wells
And of rivers, of fair meads and woods,
Of metal and of precious stones.
For there is gendered a six cornered stone,
That is to wit, Iris, that maketh a rainbow
In the air, if it be set in the sun.
And there is jet found, and white pearls.

1. NAMES

There is a cross-country echo in the names
Of Ireland's places: Ancient Kills and Raths
Planted in four provinces lead the stranger
Over the map and into the myth, in search
Of sounds: Kilkenny, Kilmeadon, Kilkee,
Kilrush, Killaloe, Kildavin, Kilpeddar. And
Rathcoole, Rathdowney, Rathkeale, Rathdrum;
Clonakilty, Crossdoney, Clonmel, and Cong;
Derrymore, Dingle, Dromartin, and Duagh;
Edenderry, Elphin, Enniscorthy, Ennis;
Shrule, Skreen, Sligo, Swinford, Straide:
Sharp and harsh, resonant and liquid names.

When you listen to the music of the names
And go from one to the other town yourself,
You will hear the names as one song and see
The towns as one town; unless there has been
Something especial, as at Kilmacanogue,
Where the bus stopped and the conductor
Leaped off in the rain to leave a bundle
Of hurleys for the Kilmacanogue team.
His agility, the splash of the puddle under
        his foot,
The strength of the grain in the fresh ash wood
Of the hurleys will leave an image in your mind.

The names become a configuration of houses,
    Roads, rains, fair weathers,
    Furze, bracken, heather,
    Turf-bogs, cliffs, downs, fogs,
    Wild flowers, wheat fields,
    Potato fields, pastureland,
    Forests, meadows, asses,
    Donkeys, horses, cattle, and sheep.
The landscape is always live and green,
And the mind dwells on it affectionately.

2. MUSIC IN THE PUB

Men of Yrlonde be singularly clothed
And unseemly arrayed and scarcely fed,
They be cruel of heart, fierce of cheer,
Angry of speech, and sharp. Nathless
They be free hearted, and fair of speech
And goodly to their own nation, and namely
Those men that dwell in woods, marshes,
And mountains. These men be pleased
With flesh, apples, and fruit for meat,
And with milk for drink: and give them
More to plays and to hunting
Than to work and travail.

The fiddle music in a Galway pub, made by
A wandering fiddler, a big young man of twenty-five,
With a handsome long face, heavy eyes, full lips,
And a shock of wet hair falling in all directions,
Is the music of a contented man whose wife
Is waiting across the road in a doorway,
Her hand resting on a pram.
This music ignores the violin and thinks
Of bells and gongs, of their mercurial overtones,
Whose quality is ancient and uncontrollable.

57

It is a lonely connection with nature,
An abridgement between music and noise,
Like the pounding of a man's heart
Under heavy stress: not music for the sake
Of music, but something ancient in the blood.
Its pulses are steady signal-beats that link
One mortal man with a long, driving line
Of ancestors, primitive, virile, commanding.

This music is never pure, logical, clean,
Mathematical, a delight to the mind
And to the senses: in this music Bach
Is yet unborn and Mozart will never be.
It is a magic of tribal communion
Which can so regulate all pulses
To the commanding heart-beat as to forge
Assorted strangers of a room into a living unit,
Oblivious of all things except the comradeship
Of being mildly drunk and mortal together
Under one roof, in one cave, at one moment,
Within the dominance of the one spell.

The bemused faces flicker with old loves
And hates; the old feet tap on the floor
To be let back in to the nimblefootedness
Of youth; or perhaps into the dancing that lies

Beyond age. But no matter how old the feet,
The music makes them dance.

Two men at a time leap up and trip about
Like gnomes, with a great mincing gaucherie
And parody of grace. They bow to each other
And slap the floor with the soles of their brogs.
And the dance, like the music that calls it forth,
Is not for the sake of dancing, but for
The propitiation of a god: the force that draws
All hearers in, to the one comradeship
  And common mortality.

3. STREET SOUNDS

Horses be joyful in fields, and smell battles,
And be comforted with noise of trumpets
To battle and to fighting; and be excited
To run with noise that they know, and be sorry
When they be overcome, and glad when they have
The mastery.

Six days of the week, the noises in Dublin streets
Have the aimless clatter and rattle of people
And animals and machines idling through

A labyrinth of desultory chores, with plenty
Of time and flexible schedules. On week-days
There are fleets of whirring bicycles and bells,
Lumbering lorries, and horses pulling milk-carts,
Bread-carts and furniture-drays. They stop
And start lazily;
                   the sound of clop-clopping hooves
Produces the gritty grind of steel-tired wheels
On the pavement, and the one sound complements
The other: the hooves explosive and echoing,
The wheels roughly hissing.
                   The regular, monotonous
Rhythm of this homely sound, familiar to man's ears
From antiquity, is not really homely at all.
It is exotic, if heard as an isolated music,
Without the benefit of sight.
                   The hooves,
Like oriental gourd-drums, resound to the
Gravelly sibilance of the weird unbreathing
Continuum given out by the wheels.
                   The sound
Of falling sand in an hour-glass, if amplified
Several thousand times, might suggest it; the soft
Sandy drift would become a mighty sibilance
Of time and space.

                    Over a cacophonous medley
Of secular sounds, clocks strike the time of day,
And bells faintly commemorate their rituals.
                    But on Sunday
Dublin street-sounds take on an air of design
And direction. They are organized, and they have
Meaning: not that of the dead, Sabbath silence
Which often pervades American towns—a suspension
Of everything, all life withdrawn indoors
And breathing privately in prostrate seclusion.
Dublin Sunday-sounds are methodical and accurate.
Most of the horses-and-carts disappear,
And the engines of accuracy for minutes at a time
Are absent altogether, leaving a background
Of quietness, upon which people hurrying
To church every hour give the effect of a population
Migrating in waves. Over this the ritual of the bells
Begins from four directions and finally gathers
Into an unbelievable counterpoint of urgencies.

The sky echoes and re-echoes with a medieval
Clangor, and the pavement resounds
With the concord of marching feet,
        Obedient to the bells.

4. THE MEDICAL HALL AND THE VICTUALLER'S IN WICKLOW

The boar is so fierce a beast, and also
So cruel, that for his fierceness
And his cruelness, he despiseth and
Setteth nought by death, and he reseth
Full piteously against the point of a spear
Of the hunter, and taketh comfort
And heart and strength for to wreak himself
On his adversary with his tusks.

At "The Medical Hall" in Wicklow you can buy
   Poultrine Fowl Powder
   Rodine Rat Poison (Fascinating and Fatal)
   Maggotine (for Sheep)
   Cooper's Warble Fly Preparation
   Cooper's Fluke and Worm Drench
And at the victualler's across the road
You can buy nothing at all, for it is night
(The summer night is still like day).

The carnal litter of sides of beef and mutton
And bloody scraps of offal after closing-time
Are hidden away for the night, and the shop

Is clean and empty as a desert. Even
The meat-cleaver has disappeared
From the chopping-block; fresh sawdust is spread
On the floor, and a bicycle stands against
One wall, like the lost relic of a forgotten
Explorer.
             In the bare windows two glossy posters
Are displayed. Both carry the same background,
A scene revealing an expanse of peaceful
Blue sky spotted with harmless clouds,
Under which stands a massive, prosperous barn
At the left; and in the meadowland at center
A number of fine cows and sheep graze
Unsuspectingly; and at the right a farmhouse
Gives off a spire of emphatic smoke. The matter
Symbolized by this scene of rural beatitude
Is printed at the bottom of the poster:

> *Humane slaughter of animals*
> *All meat supplied by us*
> *Is from Animals slaughtered*
> *With the Humane Killer.*

And on the other sign is the injunction:
             Try our noted Brawn.

5. DUBLIN DOCKS

The raven beholdeth the mouths of her birds
When they yawn. But she giveth them no meat
Ere she know and see the likeness of her own
Blackness, and of her own colour and feathers.
And when they begin to wax black, then afterward
She feedeth them with all her might and strength.

On a sunny afternoon the dry grime and blowing silt
Of the Dublin docks glitters in scattered
Diamond-points, fitful and unlovely. Between
The North Wall and Sir John Rogerson's Quay
Lies the oil-dark Liffey, sluggish and ugly.
The harbor stretches beyond, eastward, and there
The sun descends and dazzles up again
Into the harbor-sky. The air out there is luminescent
But the somnolent river, no matter how sharply
The light searches it, gives back only a dull
Thievish asphalt-colored reflection to the sun.

Tattered old men loiter along the quay,
With eyes as listless and empty of reflection
As the oily river. They see everything,
But make no sign. The loaders dawdle
Ponderously at rolling barrels up a ramp

Into a lorry. A few boat-owners, conspicuously
Spruce and smartly dressed, appraise
The squalid cargo. They are quiet as hawks,
Their eyes alert and ravenous, their faces still.
They miraculously appear and disappear.
But schoolboys going home to the tenement houses
Leap with excitement at what they find: ingots,
Lengths of railway track, bulky chains,
Rusty tanks, pieces of an iron bedstead,
Fragments of machines and motors broken beyond
Identification.
                    A silver-gray drayhorse, round
And well-fed, stands staring into the west,
The brass medallion on his bridle-gear
Spangled into a sun-burst. The drayman stops
To pick up the butt of a dead cigarette,
                    lights it
With a chunk of smouldering manila rope,
Which he tosses back to the ground. Somewhere
In the warehouse, a grinding winch or windlass
Screams out the first bars of Brahms's lullaby
Over and over like an insane throstle;
And the lorries roar and rumble away.

Into the sun, the squalor, and the din
Strolls a dark, bald-headed little man
Who wears the hair at his temples nostalgically

Drawn over the skull and plastered down
In neat wisps that no wind can disturb.

6. GALWAY

Roofs are trees areared and stretched
From the walls up to the top of the house,
And bear up the covering thereof.
And stand wide beneath, and come together
Upwards, and so they nigh nearer and nearer,
And are joined either to other in the top
Of the house. It holdeth up heling, slates,
Shingle, and laths. The lath is long
And somewhat broad, and plain and thin,
And is nailed thwart over to the rafters,
And thereon hang slates, tiles, and shingles.
The rafters are strong and square, and hewn
Plain. And are made fair within
    With fair joists and boards.

A land full of ruins; not romantic ruins
Well-kept, every angle of the broken stone
Arrested in its particular anachronism,
With the ivy trimmed, and the keeper
Nicely uniformed, collecting shillings;

But castles where cows bed in their filth,
Abandoned and gutted castles given up to cows
That graze on barren hillsides in the mists
And move like bovine ghosts into the
Horrible drawing-room at night. So it is
In the Dublin Mountains.

                      Across the island
On a Galway road that leads up
Toward the University, a cottage stands
With the roof gone, the window-glass broken;
Yet the door is securely nailed up,
As if in respect to the privacy of householders
Who have left the ashes of their fires
In the blackened chimneys. The late
Daylight falls clearly into the three rooms,
On the stone walls and the rubble and ashes
Of the floor.

              In a rainy country the sky,
Whipped by winds bringing rags and taggles
Of gray cloud over all, quickly fills up
With a rush of dull gray, the color of a mass
Of unwashed sheep's wool; and the rain
Falls on the thatched roof of the sound house
Next door and the slate roof of the house
On the other side. And it falls outrageously

Into the rooms of the cottage that has no roof,
In a land of ruins: roofless castles, towers,
Abbeys, fortresses, manor houses, cottages.

The ruin is a mnemonic of the racial consciousness,
And so it rots, given over to time.

7. GLENDALOUGH

In Ireland is a little island, in which
Men die not, but when they be overcome
With age, they be borne out of that island
To die without. In Ireland is no serpent,
No frogs, nor venemous addercop; but all
The land is so contrary to venemous beasts
That if the earth of that land be brought
Into another land, and spronge on the ground,
                    It slayeth serpents.

In Britain lived my ancestors: in England
And Scotland, some of them; and in Ireland
Lived the clan of Maoinaigh, in the year
One thousand in Galway, before that in the Mayo

Territory, and afterwards until the New World
Opened up, where they lived, God knows;
But all their bones were buried here
    Until two hundred years ago.

POEMS BY STEPHEN MOONEY

News
FROM THE SOUTH

THE UNIVERSITY OF TENNESSEE PRESS · KNOXVILLE

Some of these poems have appeared previously. Grateful acknowledgments are due the editors of the following publications: *The New Republic,* for "After Selma"; *The Georgia Review,* for "Frost"; *The New Yorker,* for "Water Color" (1958) and "The Piano Tuner" (1964) copyrighted © in the respective years shown by The New Yorker Magazine, Inc.; *The Carleton Miscellany,* for "Poetry is Percussion"; *Première,* for the part of "The Middle Age of a Traveling Salesman" which appeared in shorter and different form as "Autolycus"; the University of Alabama Press, for "Young Swimmers," first printed in *These Unmusical Days* (1951), ed. August H. Mason; *Beloit Poetry Journal,* for "The Garden," "On My Way to the Circus," and "The Guide's Speech"; and *Shenandoah,* for "Dancing in Circles," copyrighted by that publication.

Library of Congress Catalog Card Number 66–14773
Manufactured in the United States of America
by Kingsport Press, Inc., Kingsport, Tennessee
Designed by Helen Orton

FOR LOIS AND RICHARD BEALE DAVIS

> Silence, be my music. Sounds,
> Go voiceless and speak secretly
> The perfect language that surrounds
> Silence. Be my music, sounds—
> Plainsong, carols, rhyming rounds,
> All measures that must come to be
> Silence. Be my music, sounds.
> Go voiceless and speak secretly.

CONTENTS

NEWS FROM THE SOUTH